Mistaking You
for a Shower
of Summer Confetti

Words by Michael Glover

Paintings by David Hornung

Mistaking You for a Shower of Summer Confetti

www.1889books
ISBN: 978-1-915045-33-1

Other publications by Michael Glover

Poetry :

Measured Lives (1994)
Impossible Horizons (1995)
A Small Modicum of Folly (1997)
The Bead-Eyed Man (1999)
Amidst All This Debris (2001)
For the Sheer Hell of Living (2008)
Only So Much (2011)
Hypothetical May Morning (2018)
Messages to Federico (2018)
What You Do With Days (2019)
One Season in Hell (2020)
The Timely Lift-Off of the Famous Harlequin-Fish (2022)

Others :

Headlong into Pennilessness (2011)
Great Works: Encounters with Art (2016)
Playing Out in the Wireless Days (2017)
111 Places in Sheffield You Shouldn't Miss (2017)
Late Days (2018)
Neo Rauch (2019)
The Book of Extremities (2019)
Thrust (2019)
John Ruskin: an idiosyncratic dictionary (2019)
Rose Wylie (2020)
Whose? (2020)
The Trapper (2021)
Nellie's Devils and Other Stories (2022)
794 Mini Sagas (2023)
The Skittery Zipper (2023)

As editor or contributor :

Memories of Duveen Brothers (1976)
Goin' down, down, down: Matthew Ronay (2006)
Between Eagles and Pioneers: Georg Baselitz (2011)
Robert Therrien (2016)
Monique Frydman (2017)
A Garland of Poems for Christmas (2022)

For Ruth,
ever my treasure garland

Yours contumaciously, I once said,
just beyond the sea's reach,
when the gatherings had concluded
that the world was to be this, this or this.

Had you spoken foolishly
enough to expect the consequences to unspool
through all those countries still barely navigable?
I have admired your aplomb for days on end.
There has been such a reaching out from far corners.
We barely knew each other again. Who's to blame?
Will some harrumphing do to make amends?

Across certain terrains dogs still do run wild, and we know them
only for what they are, not what they might have been.
Autumn gave us the last of it, and we all bowed graciously,
just off to the left, I find myself adding gratuitously,
flexing such muscles as we knew not that we had.
Who is caught in a trap such as that one clearly was,
on days such as these? You tell me that, you say,
in answer to my queries, that is, in order to humour me.
Is it good to be gay together again or not at all?
I have asked myself that repeatedly,
when the evening has loured down upon us
like those long and heavy drapes
your mother had so insisted upon, and repeatedly,
suffocating the best of us, of which there were once so many.
Now barely any at all. Who would have guessed,
all paper fragility that we are and must surely forever be,
that we were once even capable of surviving
such a barrage of barrel bombs in the end,
with only our eyes left strewn about haphazardly
to express consternation or surprise?

The dusty streets once again are chock full of Picasso
mustering his Saltimbanques into the usual visual routines.
When will such familiarity decline into tedium? I vainly ask.
for one say we have now reached that point, so do your best

1

not to contradict me again, my dear old antagonist…
How sad they all look, and in exchange for how little?
He gave them crumbs from a paper bag, and the littlest –
I saw it with my own eyes – kicked him in the butt.
What's to be done with us when a painter like him
gets mistreated in such a variety of ways –
which must include, I assume, evidence of extreme success
so readily granted? I am tired of too many questions.
Just let me sleep again in the long bed, the one you bought
at whim, without any consultation with me.
Had you not even measured my legs? Did you not see me?
I have seen myself at last. It happened only yesterday, I confess,
and I felt neither fear nor surprise when it happened because
I had overheard myself being discussed so often
and in such a bewildering variety of situations.
Do I surprise you with that news?
Had you expected me by now to be over-familiar with myself
at the very least, and to the point of tedium? Well then.
The sleeve has been cut down the middle
with such skill, deftness and aplomb,
and you claim, as you generally do, that you were not watching.
Life for you then must forever remain a perpetual surprise,
jocund and leaping as any fine tuned, fine sprung Elizabethan lyric.
I have caught you at your guessing game, my friend,
and you have no ready answer because
you are lost to me in the wilds of your manifold stories of success.

How did we find each other? It is all such an improbable story
that I, frankly, have no wish to repeat, but especially
when the sun has once again graced us with its favours
(this being the middle of June), so let us return to the subject
of the fluidity of water, and of how it rolls across
and then slips between the finger joints when you pour it
directly from the bottle, from above. I have asked for no favours,
and the world, having stared hard at this gage thrown down,
has chosen to respond with a variety of answers,
each one of them mutually exclusive.
Let us then think together of Great Saint Mary's

2

on any morning of early summer, when you have just walked
in front of me for a second time, expecting,
by your headlong gait, a future of sorts to happen,
though anticipating, by the cool blankness
of your look, nothing much at all.
Is Browning in my pocket that morning,
with his clumsy running rhythms?
Why should I bother even to ask such questions?
There are such distances to cover, almost all at once,
let alone entire passing worlds of weariness.
The far prospect of youthfulness is always a bore,
as are other statistics. The world exists only to be yawned over.
Let us take that for a truth, and then pass quickly on.
This habitation known only to me must remain
a riddle for as long as the body still runs, as it must,
though not for much longer, you tell me.
The diseases must come and go.
You blink and they are here, freshly to be spoken of,
before they disappear again, hiding behind the sofa,
in front of which the promise of noon sings out, and we all
rise to the occasion, as we always must until we do not.

There is too much candour in the air, too much
crisp, light singing of the kind which never fails to bemuse
and annoy. Snip it off, make it all go away with exaggerated
wafts of the hand and other assorted sillinesses.
Let the body stand here alone with its tediums
and its futile speculations. There is so little left to be fought over.
The buildings once here, so fine and so perky of their kind,
have been rased in their entirety, you may have noticed.
We are being encouraged to salute a new reality.
Sense impressions are the meagrest part of it.
Be gone then. Salute the promise of every second brother
as a wayfaring stranger. Choose amongst all past lives
the one you would most dearly wish to describe
you were offered that ticket, and then chose to accept it.
Pick about in this stream with a childhood stick,
and haul him up for prolonged interrogation. You surely must.

He will be ready. He will not disappoint
if your questions – and this may be the catch –
do not disappoint. There is so little else left to amuse
or preoccupy us at the bottom of the garden.
Many were the moments, were they not?

It is too late to regret that the ticket was lost.
No apologies are applicable – or even recognisable.
It is all so makeshift as you throw a left
down and down into the city.
You have no idea where you are. None of the
signage makes sense. All you see ahead, through the miasma,

is an outline of shapes, which rise and fall in no particular order,
looming and then just as quickly withdrawing.
The descent continues – down, down, down –
because the invitation was general.
Yes, there is no mistaking it. This is the place.
This is the opening you applied for.
You have dressed for the occasion – black, grey,
and even a chancy flash of yellow at the neck.
The words are on your lips, every last little foolishness.
This is your pledge, your promise, your hope, you murmur,
genuinely comforted by listening to the words of reassurance
that you repeat over to yourself.
Nevertheless, no matter what you judge your age to be,
you are still a blundering, faltering child
who is capable of controlling almost nothing.
This, in the mind, is a tree, for example. You go to touch it.
You scratch it with your nails, doing yourself harm,
at which you mewl. You had not expected.
You had not anticipated such a harsh reprisal.
You know only the little that you know.
Can it ever be enough? If you were to write to yourself,
would that help? Would you thereby
thicken your understanding of this situation?

This is the least that there is to be seen.
It has been whittled down at last.
That is an advantage, of course – there is no
further to fall. We have hit rock bottom.
The extent of every last disappointment is soon to be known –
or perhaps it is here already, and you had not
quite recognised it for what it is.
(Limitations must always be a part of the story.)
There are grapes on the table, in the glass calyx
usually reserved for flowers of joy and abundance,
and you go to gather a small bunch
of them in your hand. You eat them with the
eagerness that grapes always seem to propose.
Momentarily, you are alive again

in a world which entirely consists of
the sweetness of grapes, and all that grapes give,
so unstintingly, so open-handedly, so unjudgementally,
to rich or to poor, without favour or discrimination.

Regrettably, the rats are back at the entrance,
dressed in their usual variants of spivishness.
Is life then to be so joyless? There was yes and then yes
again, way back when, as we said before we were unhorsed
at the back of the privy and other vulgarities.
How to accommodate such drawling?
Did you not, at least for once in your life,
grow weary of it all, and even scratch a plea
for freedom across the butter?
Would you say that we counted for nothing?
I for one snatched at everything within reach,
the highs and the lows of it all. We were never
wanting for a bough, you would have said
with the usual sickening weight of confidence.
How though to define us now?
Could you even begin to guess? The saloon
bar is full of us again, as you try to escape
through the window, I watching you go,
blowing the usual kisses of farewell
and regret for it all. Those songs, welling up
from the back of the throat, were always so many.
We, on the other hand, were always perhaps too few
when it came to the count, as it always must.
I grant you that and nothing more.
I grant you so little that you must surely disappear
if the wind shifts in its appointed direction,
which risks being the last of our futile fantasies.
I grant you a swell of luck the equal of your measure.
And where does that get us? I hear you ask,
as if you are trumpeting yet another beach holiday,
with the towels draped so lazily across the arm of the chair,
which has already slumped with a sigh
into time's slow shifting sands, ho jolly hum.

Would you be me if you were invited to choose?
Or would you prefer to be yourself after all,
bright at the doorway as a bird peeking out of its nest
before wresting a worm from futurity's sharp beak?
Where did we go to? Did we merely vanish
for no particular reason other than that we were being
questioned closely about our vanishing intentions,
and had taken suitable umbrage?
How would we have known? Not I. Not you.
Never you because you generally chose not to.
The ferment has since gone on forever,
and no one holds it back because, frankly, no one cares.
That is the long and the short of it –
I am of course dealing here in various lengths
of yellow ribboning of the kind that she wore
to embellish her dress at the party
at which she always looked so lovely
precisely because there were no rivals.
In fact, no one was present at all if you choose
to discount all the bottles, which were always so eager
to make things happen, poor, lonely hospitable things…

There was no door to be opened,
and there never had been according to the rule book.
I had tried before, many times, and you tried after me.
We cried over it all day. The tools had vanished.
To be entirely truthful, we had never quite
bought the tools in the first place,
and the door had always been a makeshift affair
because you or I – one of us, surely –
had never wanted to spend the money that it costs
to buy a portal or a threshold,
which was exactly what was needed,
given the gravity or the sacredness of the situation.
When will it all come right? When will the plumb line
work again? It is all so simple a matter,
simple as cutting water with a pair of scissors,
that line straight down and through,

at which I have always been so adept
because you have seen me do it,
day after hard won day you have watched me.
It has always been my favourite party trick,
that and choosing between one convicted felon and another
in order to ascertain the gravity of the situation
in this village, which had never known such tumult until now.
Am I making myself clear to you?
Was it like this before? Am I being clear as new splashed water?
Or is this fresh predicament something
of our own making, which we have wanted for so long
that we have cried buckets of regret and longing over it?
I am acquainted only with on-screen tears,
when lights are dimmed and fingers fumble across
whole acres of pop corn, and we leave, refreshed,
With the light having long since fallen,
to streets newly embodying the mysteries of evening.
It is all such a long story to be told,
but that is quite enough of it for one brief interlude
of misery, not readily to be shared more fully.

Are you still here with me?
Did they drag it all down in the end,
heartless as beasts with throats slit so deftly?
And are all the flats gone too, bent from the rain
beating down at a slant, pummelling the side of that wall
without forethought or mercy?
Were they even acquainted with those words?
Well then! Let God be judge and uprooter in one.
What a child's picture book of desolation!
Of curious interest too though, it has to be said,
because somewhere there is a watcher
who must surely be gaining ground
just off to the edge of the picture.
That, at least, is my angle of view,
and I am obliged for just as long
as I go on talking in this way
to be faithful to myself

if you choose to continue to follow
the silken thread of this argument…

After the flour is kneaded,
it remains in the bowl, minding its own business,
having carefully set aside all issues of contentment,
and knowing nothing of philosophical generalities,
until the time arrives – having skipped a section or two –
for us to eat it with confidence,
and at that point the bread too becomes
roundedly and swellingly philosophical.
Would you not agree?
Are there other, better ways to wake you?
And, if so, could you go as far as to recommend one or two,
should you ever rise up on your elbow again?

When new light is framed by a window,
good, wholesome light

of the kind to be encouraged,
even the least and most wasted of us
choose at that moment to walk towards it,
dreamy and somnambulistic.
Nothing is said. No words are exchanged.
There is nothing to *be* said.
It is merely a minimal response
to a gesture of welcoming
of which we had quite forgotten
any new day to be capable
until that moment.
What then happens next?
Can it be spoken of?
And if the curtains are fully drawn back,
by even the clumsiest of hands,
What then, what then?
Will there be roaring?
Will there be lamentation?
Will there be seeing to be reported?

Or off to the left a little.
Yes, make it all shapeless.
That is as silly as it gets –
pardon, that is as silly as *you* get.
The barometer in the corner
makes the first wish of many,
and you are thankful for that.
You even make a pledge to buy it
when solvency restores you to humanity
in those weeks and months ahead.

Crass as your last wish.
There was a pile-up, and few survived
the telling of that tragedy,
which continued for weeks.
Rouge was added to the palest of cheeks,
knuckles brought back into play,

and you guessed everything
that there was to be guessed.
Who could lose?
Least of all you
who must never be accused
of infantilism at best.

Caught short in the aftermath.
The way that grey sings across the water.
Did you ever hear me when I told you that?
There was too much junketing, always,
and the lemons were only ever partially squeezed.
Turn on the tap to feed all this abundance
until the day it all turned sallow again
and we were down on our knees in the kitchen,
looking again again for…feverfew, was it?
Goodness knows what.
I caught you out again that Monday
when the knapsack was at the ready.
It's only the regular routine, you quothed,
as you left so breezily, and the floor, of course,
needed to be scraped clean.
Had you ever thought of ordeals as such
on any day we might be counting?
I am in my seventh heaven, you said.
Thanks for the good tidings, I replied,
neither wishing you well nor otherwise.
It was just the way things fell out in our country.
In short: another lame-duck affair
with the usual eventualities limping along after.

And now all the words are clean again,
brushed off, combed out, nothing ratty or makeshift any more.
I go about my business like any good shoe-shine boy.
I also know where you kept the hat stand
as if your life depended on it,
and how laboursome it is to carry about
so much lost or discarded emotion.

You'd agree with that at least.
I can't take you any other way
because the opening has always been
at the top corner, en route to the attic,
where darkness takes it time from noon on (or thereabouts).
Wriggle your finger around. Sure as hell,
you'll find it soon enough if you are serious about such matters.
Do I trust you to do the necessary?
Are you still out in the garden anyway,
Coat half buttoned up, fuming characteristically?
Why did you always want to go go go so soon after arriving?
Was it never enough for you, what got laid out on the plate,
I mean all the usual abundance?
Why so queasy all the time,
as if nothing was ever quite right for you?
Who takes a tape measure to a mouse,
and then laughs it off as if nothing
had ever been expected of you?
You disgust me, with your oozy, posthumous dealings,
always so frantic and ignoble.
No one taught you good manners,
least of all your mother,
that's what it amounts to,
and you still – still! – do not want to hear me say it
because it's an affront to all your stupid pettinesses, isn't it?
The larder was only ever good for cold things –
I mean keeping them cold in there
for as long as it takes to ignore them.
We did it side by side, it was always the same routine.
Not least, because your mouth hung open.
Were you always that comic-book person?
The question is always worth the asking in my humble opinion.
You know how powerfully I muse upon such ape-shit things
as if all our lives depended upon it – well, mine at the very least.
Then, an hour or two on from the barbecue,
when everyone was lying around looking wounded or neglected,
you kicked out with your left leg again,
and did your usual monkeying around

for hours on end – or so it seemed to my jaundiced eye.
How much of a diversion *was* that then,
do you honestly believe,
just before the lightning struck the guardian
and sent us all scurrying?
You wouldn't have had it any other way though.
You needed to act out the usual range of lame fantasies.
Why should it not be said? What is the merit of all this silence?
If I am to be charged with writing all this down,
why not get on with it and damn the consequences?
Because, frankly, things couldn't be worse than they are,
could they? If I had survived, you now wheeze,
it could have got a little better,
with patience and the unexpected gift
of a little more money.
I'm thoroughly ashamed of you now.
In fact, I may even wind up what amounts
to nothing more than a lame dribble of a conversation.

You thought once you had me in a box.
I sprung out. I pointed. I jabbed and I jeered at you.
We knew so little of each other back then.
I had even called for it, I believe:
a delicious experiment of a wholly unexpected nature.
That was then. Words change their meanings.
Worlds get upended. Leaves get swept away
by that dogged crone with the broom
from the valley's bottom
whom we tipped so handsomely because she
always struck such a pose.
Enough of her! What of me though?
This is why I am writing at all,
don't you quite understand that?
needn't have been so extreme.
could have sat here clutching this bottle
and remained silent for years.
No one would have noticed.
No one would have expected anything else of me

13

because you are what you are
to the random observer, aren't you?
No one in his right mind
chooses to interrogate a stone.
The fact is that I wanted you for myself
because I sensed a profound inner incompletion.
No one wanted to listen to me in those days.
No one suggested that I organise my words
in any particular order.
I was at a loss with what to do with my life.
And then, one day,
you were standing outside the door,
cool as a lemon slice on a side plate,
and I took a little nibble out of you.
Were you sour? Of course you were!
Which added to the interest of course.
And the next time I looked, the plate was empty,
and I had to buy an entire sack of lemons
from the greengrocer just to find you.
I jest of course. You hadn't gone away
because you needed a roof over your head.

There was no road at all for years.
It just disappeared. That was fine though.
We had no inclination to go anywhere.
The food arrived from the sky, in wicker baskets
that groaned beneath the weight, all let down by pulleys.
How did they do such a thing?
And why do it anyway?
Were we an experiment of some kind?
Was somebody eager to assess the outcome?

Who cares? We had not a care in the world
for years and years,
when life just kept coming and coming.
Were you in my pocket or was I in yours?
It just seemed not to matter.
We were so in love with the ease and the serenity of it all.

Days, weeks, hours, minutes – who was awake
or alert enough to care? It was all this
gently lulling continuum. Such blessings.
And then one morning I became fixated by
your angularity when you bent over
to wash out the tooth mug.
He disgusts me, I found myself mouthing.
He is to be absent from my gaze,
I found myself muttering with subdued,
though perfectly calibrated, malevolence.
I had given the order almost without thinking –
some inner compulsion had driven it out –
and at that moment you vanished.
You were gone from my sight, never to return again.

Is this a weapon to be treated with caution?
Or am I to drool all over it, call it,
with great and uncharacteristic tenderness,
my especial darling?
I am at a loss to know what to do.
I am at a loss to be anyone else,
someone, for example, who owns such a thing.
Butter is far better as a topic of conversation,
everyone is eager to talk about butter
because it has neutrality written all over it.
And I have danger written all over me.
My cheeks flush. My fists clench.
My words spill forth in every direction at once.
No one wants me. Fortunately, I fascinate myself.
I understand how to please myself,.
I recognise when I need to be fed,
and what foodstuffs will surely delight me –
milk and bananas, and the wholesome aroma
of freshly baked bread, for example. So far so good.

The consequence is that I have proceeded with my life.
Generally speaking, I have gone about,
beaten the bounds of this parish, unimpeded.
There have been stray dogs and rats, of course.
No world is complete without a smattering
of verminous matter.
I have taken it all in my stride. I have worn high-sided boots.
I have called on a stout stick to be my faithful companion,
and it has never disappointed me.

Now there is little else to be known because, frankly,
I have studied too hard and too long.
I have run after the Phantom of All Knowledge
until completely spent and breathless.
And it has all been very good for me.
I feel like a form which has been filled out.
No gaps, no missing answers. No lies.
No awkward shufflings of the feet

when confronted by the long shadow of Authority.
All crisp, clean, clear and straightforward.
I jest of course. The opposite has been true.
I am talking of a life of fantasy,
that life I once perhaps hoped to live,
that life I might once have wished
to conjure for myself, almost from nothing.
Not any longer. Truth is best,
and the truth of life is always baleful.
It is short and it is bitter.
It comes and it goes at remarkable speed.
What time for reflection? No time.
There is only the little that is this,
these few meagre words of reportage,
which are almost always worthless
because they encompass so little.
Most of it fleets by, too quick to be seen or judged.
I wish that this were not so, but it is. It is.
And there is no remedy but death,
which is the sweetest thing imaginable
when you are not yet dead yourself,
and the idea of it swims by yet again,
does it not, just then, at that moment of passing,
as it waves so nonchalantly out from the car
with the white-gloved right hand,
seeming like a pleasing and plausible proposition?

t struck a note so high and so clear.
The road leaned westerly,
which seemed like the way to go,
or all of us, and all at once –
uch congestion! Such heave-ho!
This is the appointed lot.
he measure is narrow,
nd not readily to be fathomed.
 tent may do. Or two.
 entirely depends upon the weather
 the quality of our conversation

as we lean out into the wind,
refreshed for a change,
wanting for nothing – or so it seems,
momentarily. Always very useful.
What age were you when it happened?
I am, needless to say, as I have always been,
telling myself the same catalogue of untruths
to whoever chooses to listen.
This garden, for example, is always
boundlessly content to attend to such whisperings.
The high day was only yesterday, do you not remember?
Have you forgotten everything then?
Am I still to count you amongst my many friends
even though you are long dead?
The dead, I have discovered,
are always the best of friends.
Their reputations are so malleable,
their attitudes unchanging,
each walk the same as it has always been.
I would run there myself,
kicking the dust off my heels as I fleet by,
were I not in conversation with you until the end.
I cannot depend upon you listening to me.
That continues to be a source of acute anxiety.
You were never a good listener.
Even your replies gave no proof incontrovertible
that you were responding to
what I had just said to you.
We chose the branch line that afternoon
because of the way it seemed to lean away from the sea
in a long, slow, genial curve.
We were walking abreast of each other.
You were so eager to go on and on,
always a little faster,
whereas I had always wanted to linger,
if not lie in wait, for what would, in time, eventuate.
Proof, then, of incompatibility,
proof that you would leave me in the end by dying

in that unseemly fashion of which I no longer wish to speak.
The city, I would always say, never loses its
headlong appetite for adventure, does it?
You had a way of avoiding me
by not speaking back when spoken to.

The lady turned away, and the room turned with her.
I had been the last to leave for a change,
which means that I saw it all.
There had never been such a dawn –
such giddiness, such adventure.
Life as yet unspoken for!
There were so many two-by-twos, constantly passing,
as if naming themselves,
as if reaching out for appreciation,
and appreciate them we did.
Who would ever want it to be otherwise?
their glances seemed to suggest.
At last, when I could no longer bring myself to reach out,
I took up a small pocketbook and committed
all of the recent past to memory,
every last word of it, the least sigh or shuffle.
And these lines are the fruits of all that labour.
Is it sweet? Are we as compatible as I had hoped?
Do tell me. Do not hold back.
Do not sink into torpor.
Do not hesitate to pronounce upon
such evidence of intimacy.
The rooms are always so spacious,
and the invited know their names
without having to be called.
They rise up from their seats when the cloudscape shifts,
floating free when the anchor begins to rust.
It is that simple, that inevitable,
not so much an outcome as a destiny.
You are familiar with that word.
You embraced it as a child, as did I,
even before I saw you.

There was no need for any introduction.
Elaboration never became us.
We were so deeply embedded in our lives
that our progress (I call it that by some inner compulsion),
freshly twinned and then blessed by the stars,
was almost bound to be inevitable.
It was that simple to those who could see,
of whom there were many,
of whom there are still so many,
though I would hesitate to name them.

Ask and it shall be granted.
The car had pink fins, needless to say,
and you barely touched the wheel
as we progressed along the parkway.
All those piggeries came later,
and we accustomed ourselves to the stench

much in the way that one learns to dress slightly differently.
I had expected a special atmosphere on that day,
but there was merely ignorance abroad again,
and a new chill in the air.
In fact, say it: roaring and rampancy everywhere.
Winter was stealing upon us.
Do I regret having missed so much,
so many days, together with evidence,
discovered so much later,
of all those balmy months?
Not really.
Hold hands to the bitter end and then beyond.
That is all there is to it.
Also, a glass of herbal tea has been known to console.

Makeshift duties, as you once remarked.
The phrase has remained, but not its context.
So much fades if you lose concentration.
The food, with its range of aromas,
disappears from the plate
almost as if it knew
that you had not the wherewithal
to pay for it on that day
of truly exceptional indigence.
The sheer tomfoolery of waiters!

Or the waiting must end.
We know that for a fact,
you in your corner and I in mine,
scraping a living of sorts,
peeling the potatoes with uncharacteristic passion
as we wait for the engines to arrive,
doing our usual obeisance next to the carpet
as mother comes and goes, pest as usual,
for all that we have loved her unto death.
How could that not be so?
The world, after all, is an impromptu affair,
the less said about that the better.

Could you even begin to describe
our predicament now,
With the two of us so disconsolate,
corridor-haunters all, for this day at least?
I have only so many summed days
at my disposal – are you still doing the counting?
I would like to say it again, now,
that I love you and have loved you,
but all this pressure of fresh spilled words
is holding me back for a change.
Let that be change in the back pocket, I mean.
You would countenance nothing less,
all being so casually macaronic.
Did I ever ask you to comment upon these words?
Well then, hang on to your place at the back
lest worse befall you tomorrow.
In the aftermath. In case of eventualities –
that kind of situation, I ask you,
when so little seems to matter any more,
and you are once again pretending
that a lifetime of talking
will see you through,
at least as far as the holly tree
abandoned at the back of the garden.

Is it to be brotherly?
Or something else altogether different?
I didn't recognise you in the latest photograph.
The light source, I guess,
has always been dubious in your snicket,
and you were always ready to hazard so little.
I, on the other hand… You finish it.
Isn't it your prerogative, you tell me,
to take matters in hand today
and call all the shots
as if you owned the place again,
my dear old roustabout?
I'm done with teasing.

When the world squats on the edge of the couch,
who wouldn't wish to be here to know
that the game's finally up,
that we're all, to put it succinctly, kaput, old friend?

It was that daub of maroon that got me going,
the way it seemed to be staring back at me,
so shamelessly, from your lapel, so cheerlessly too.
It was then that I lost heart.
It was then that I finally said to myself:
go home, try a different routine altogether.
The best of your gags is exploded.
You're nothing but a pretence at human feeling.
So I gave up the ghost for a day or two.
At least I said I did. No one else was there even to notice.
I could have got away with anything,
any way to live my life would have done
in such awkward and unprecedented circumstances.

Who? What? Why though? Did you ask those questions?
Impossible! I keep telling you that you are dead,
and no longer have the capacity to intervene
in the way that you used to.
Your bow, together with that quiver of arrows,
got flung into the fire's back
with an encouraging yelp, way back when.
Remember now? Remember just how childish
you were that morning, shivering there, naked,
trying to hold on to your modesty,
and keep yourself warm too, it being the dead of winter,
close to the very centre of what was once always
described in our school books as the Low Countries,
all that flatness stretched out today and forever,
all that carrying from dyke to dyke of
sackfuls of Delftware in the hope that
we might begin again? It never did.
All your arrows are spent, my friend.

This is the measure of it all.
This is why we have decided to stand still
and count all the bean counters again
until it all falls away into a shower of summer confetti,
and love gets played once again on the radio at home,
where you rise to the occasion,
pulling your old grey socks up, up a little higher
until they entirely cover over
those bruisings of the ankle bone
from which you suffered for so long –
until, that is, the 'miracle cure' happened,
and you slotted yourself back into the world –
just as if you had re-found your own space
in that packet of biscuits we all love to love so.

You are a success by any and every worldly measure,
and we do rate you for that.
We have even given you back all your due,
everything that had ever been stolen from you
in the days of retribution, when morals
were so much slime finger-raked down a wall,
and we all walked the straight and narrow,
hunched into our jackets,
praying that all would soon end,
and it did, of course, when the book was finally closed,
and the last and best pages burnt for fire wood –
who would ever have guessed
that paper pulp could be so thick and unyielding?

I am making none of this up, you understand.
I believe in the truthfulness of these words,
as you surely must too
or nothing can begin again at all,
we will both be at a loss,
not even knowing whether this bus stop,
at which I am waiting so patiently,
is the terminus or not.
Things could prove that bad between us,

so let us cling to this hope of ours,
this shared and cherished hope,
as one dutifully clings to
the miserable remnant of yesterday's sandwich.

Walking helps. It helps a lot.
We have both tried it, have we not?
(Excuse me?) Drifting apart a little way –
or hand in hand, mingling sweat so pleasingly.
And then there is the way in which the Earth,
(I capitalise it in that way to show reverence,
calling it by that simple act *hallowed ground*),
as if knowing we are here,
beats solemn time beneath our feet,
welcoming our footfalls,

and the more difficult the terrain,
the more spiritual the experience…
Did you not find that too?
We must talk about it when we have a moment.

When I watch a log being split in half,
it is as if the brain has fallen apart,
that painful, that alarming.
I get others to do my chopping for me.
To stay in the parlour with my games of chance –
all those ivory figures shifting here and there
across a chequered board –
this is my preference these days,
my style of ballroom dance you might even say,
when so much has drawn back,
and the world feels so fearful.
There were so many once,
far too many according to many,
now there are just two or three
and the vocabulary is so limited.
I try to toss in, for old times' sake,
the odd verbal extravagance,
but so few seem to care or even notice.
It is as if I simply do not exist any more.
I do exist because I am writing all this to you
and you are listening to me,
showing your usual level of tolerance
or perhaps it is indulgence
because although you do not especially like me
you are not quite ready to be wholly rid of me
because we two are two of so few, is that not true?
Did I not just say so?
Well then.

Pass the jar along the table.
Slide it – if it will go.
Show a little charity for a change.
You have been buttoned up for far too long.

You do not even use the word in my presence,
not any more. The word jar is no longer a part
of our common currency.
Is that why you tore off the label just now,
to dehumanise the object,
to make it a little easier to ignore my requests?

There were inches once.
Between finger and thumb you could catch one,
as if you were trapping a fly. That satisfying.
No longer speak of such matters.
Regularise the little that we do,
the less that we see.
That makes it all tolerable.
It gives life a limitedly pleasing shape.
Pare back. Strip back
until each bone is a nonentity

to be usefully ignored.
Nothing to be challenged.
Nothing to be asked for.
Nothing to be gainsaid.
No questions requiring an ultimate answer.
That is where we should aim, obviously,
and you must surely agree:
towards the balm of oblivion.

I used this phrase once,
if not on multiple occasions:
Yours Sincerely.
And I deployed those words sincerely.
At least I believed that to be true –
as far as I am able to remember
the quality and the honesty of my past responses.
These are such vexing matters.
One thing gets heaped upon another,
and the outcome is always so lumpish, so shapeless.
You cannot even comfortably sit on it.
And one does get so tired at day's end.
One does so want to sit on it,
if only to silence it, and put it in its place.
Otherwise, there would be such randomness
out loose in the air, and one would spend one's time
idly snatching here, there and everywhere.
Who would know when to begin or end?
Who would ever recover from the exhaustion of it all?
I find such a question unanswerable – as do so many.
I know that you agree with me
because today, given the balminess of the weather,
you are in a mood to humour me,
in part at least, because I have pleased you.

Did it ever happen before?
Just the once, did I hear you say,
when the weather was its usual restrictive self,
and we had walked in from the rain,

damp-necked, and with so little to live for
that you had thrown your jacket down onto the floor
even though we had not been arguing that morning,
not especially, by my recollections of such matters?
Frankly, I am tired of posing so many questions.
You are a model of obtuseness, always have been.
Let me take it all back then, and walk away.
The city is beckoning me again.
Nothing is too far from my aspirations of good cheer.
When I walk into the cafe, so many smiles will be turned
upon me. I shall feel good about myself.
The table will be wiped clean of tobacco ash
with a deft swipe of the waiter's cloth,
he who has always loved me,
and makes my coffee just as I want it.
Nothing will be wanting.
Life will no longer feel like a haunting.
The fence line is over there, by the way,
I hear you insistently saying,
no longer listening to anything that I tell you,
and, yes, I have indeed posed for the snap once again,
just as you asked, remember.
No one ever enquired of me whether *I* wanted
to wear such a jacket on a Thursday.
It was all one long imposition.
The wheels still turn all right,
but so much more slowly, grindingly so,
and I am always waiting for something to happen.
Is this a good space to be occupying?
Would you blame me if I were to protest out loud?
Try this thumb-nail sketch of the neighbourhood
as we used to know it before it all went wrong.
I have added a deal of blurry, eggy sunlight
to make it look all the more enticing.
You recognise all the neighbours, of course,
by which I mean that you are almost bound to ignore them
because that is what you do, and have always done.
In the interim, there were hours such as these,

which always felt so exquisite because
fragments of magic were forming off to the edge,
before we had even begin to listen or to notice.
It is a little like being drunk all over again
on a Sunday morning, and hearing nothing
but the tolling bell of a thunderous head.
I sometimes wish it were not like this.
There is no word the equal of cataclysm,
but I for one would not have the gall to deploy it
because I was not born on that side of the bed.
You heaved me off, right back to where
the town took on hints of countryside again.
I recognised nothing of where I was.
I had no wish to have any of this repeated
because I knew already everything
that was due to be said of me,
up to and beyond the outer limits,
and none of it was pretty or to my taste.

To be entirely inconsequential once again,
have you ever tasted a lemon posset?
I have had two or three, in quick succession,
and they were all quite delicious.
Such a matter has just engulfed my thinking.
You alone would understand for what reason
I drool in this way, with so little else to attend to.
You made me what I am, do not pretend otherwise.
There are hard choices to be made,
and all my neighbours have made a decision
to shift the street lights to the other end of the neighbourhood,
as if darkness were wholly incompatible with unreason.
I jest of course. I am a funny man.
This is why being is the older part of seeming.
It has always been that way.
You wanted such fogs of goodness out in the air.
You listened then. You chose to attend
to every last, least particular
on the days when I slept like a child,
needing and wanting for nothing.
Solitary children always make their way back home.
Solitary children carry the biggest begging bowls.
Solitary children have eyes to see with
for a very limited period of their lives.
That was a little song of my childhood.
I was invited to recognise myself in it.
Needless to say, I refused. I broke the glass instead,
and waited for answers in the privet hedge,
which were slow to come.
It was there that I grew to be a man.
I would have preferred to be a tree, needless to say,
but the opportunity was not presented to me.
Can there be much more?
Is there not too much already?
Summer's end was the poignant moment.
It was then that I felt fully lifted
out of myself and beyond,
readied to begin the next journey.

Whispering takes up hours in plenty,
all that you had not yet told yourself,
strategies of avoidance to be mindful of.
It is the beginning of all worldliness.
To count the self whole has always been the danger.
Look out for such an hour.
Never slacken or loosen the belt.
Be the robber, if not the pretender.
That door opens on to greater opportunities than most.
I hear you nod in agreement.
Let me shake your hand
and call you a brother – just for the sake of it.
Or there is much else that we could talk about.
Was it not you who once said
that the vistas were limitless to such as ourselves?
You may have. You may have not.
Have it all ways. So much has fallen away.
So much now seems even to contradict what it always was.
And then, well, what's left after that?
We do keep on asking and asking,
just as once there were answers
to which we might just be privy by and by,
the wind not necessarily blowing
in the right direction for matters
so demonstrably demonic, my sometime friend.
I for one prefer marmite with my toast,
though I have always had a penchant for breakfast.
Food is a hard decision, when it is not just off to the edge,
as you tend to be in these dog days of your persistence.
Would you have spoken of yourself in such a way?
I doubt it. Let me then do it for you.
I am happy to assist with the heavy lifting,
being a man amongst men once again.
Did you ever have an appetite for pleasure?
Is that how I might define you?
Your angles were always so many, and shifting.
This might have been as much as needed to be said,
were I not still obliged by my very cussed nature

to confront you every minute god sends.
Has it all really been a catastrophe?
That and a little more,
a dessert on the side would you say,
were I ever to ask you,
which I would not of course dream of doing.
This is all my game, and I play it
at the speed it invites. Your move now.

When we eventually spoke to the taxidermist,
he pulled a face which seemed to suggest
that some hawks are beyond reprieve or repair,
and we merely had to accept it
by drinking far more than we should have
for any common-or-garden working Thursday.
It is the way things happen.
You cannot push it aside – inevitability, I mean.
Respond as you must. Yours to be doing
and undoing – the usual unhelpful posturing.
And then, of course, there is the unrelieved
plainness of it all, why such colours keep on returning
with such persistence. I had not asked for them.
Grey is not a favourite of mine.
I have seldom been privy to your thinking,
which is what of course keeps me interested
and buoyant in the teeth of adversity.
I have made myself what I am.
I sat in this carriage (second-class),
and then quite pointedly refused to budge
when the ticket collector bore down on me,
and then proceeded to remind me
of a multitude of vices – that the ticket was invalid,
for example; that I was still too young to travel
unaided on my own in clothes quite as loud as
the ones I was wearing, and so it went on.
I have forgotten all the rest.
The list stretched as far as the dinky little Hamlet of Tedium
and then way beyond, believe me because
I am not yet the dependable liar
that I may yet in time become,
with a little study and a little patience.
I simply do not know how it has all happened.
All was set fair in my childhood.
I knew no wrong. Nothing went amiss.
My father had his pipe and his chair (leatherette),
and a long and far-seeing look,
which I later – much later, it has to be said –

came to admire. That is as much as needs to be said.
There is always too much,
and I have no wish to commit it all to paper
because I am not that sort of a person.
I am this sort of a person, twice as honest
as the day is long, and days do lengthen, on and on,
during these balmy summer months,
so you must agree to settle down here
and trust me for as far and as long
as we need to travel together.
Understood? Happy? Well belted in?
Let us then continue without further interruption.

I had made it clear to you, from the start,
That things could proceed like this,
smoothly and agreeably,
provided that you did not make
unreasonable demands upon my patience,
which from time to time you have striven to do,
and I have done my best to ignore you.
Let it settle then. Nothing will be coming at you
bullishly. It will be as if you had almost anticipated
everything that I was going to tell you,
that my story was to be your story in the end,
which might have been perfectly possible
f we two had forever been as one,
which of course we are not, and never have been.
What excitement would there have been
n discovering that it was not even possible to insert
he width of a sheet of paper between us?
 am at a loss even to contemplate such an outcome.
No such conversation as this one would have been possible.
The point is that you do not know
exactly what it is that I am about to say,
nd, were you to know in advance –
y means of a transcript, for example –
ou would not even be listening, would you?
ll perfectly fair and understandable, my friend.

And don't you pretend otherwise.
I know you through and through.
You can be too tricksy for your own good
when the moment seizes you.

Is there a light from that window?
Or is it merely another reflection
of the kind which happens
when you attach a sheet of paper
coated with silver foil or similar
to a surface, and then beam a bright light at it?
Is it, in short, the moon that I can see over there
or another species of illusion?
I would welcome your contribution.
On matters philosophical,
you choose to remain silent.
You sit there like an unstuffed and unappealing
sack, giving back nothing,
not even having the grace
to face in my direction
because you have better or more urgent
matters to attend to. Or perhaps it is
that you are asleep
and will not wake up again until the tide turns –
or some other humbug.
You do test my patience.
When we were young together,
I would always run on ahead
for the sheer joy of exercising my legs.
It did not occur to me then, being young and foolish,
that you were holding back, dragging your feet,
to make a point. What exactly *was* that point though?
Even now I do not know,
even now, when I stare into your face (as I do now),
I see only a blank or a knowing smirk,
as if you have already outwitted me on some point
which will forever remain unclear to me.
Why would you do such a thing, then or now?

Why would you hold back in this way,
as if you knew that perfection
would and could never be a part of
our prolonged and difficult engagement?
You remain unfathomable to me,
forever deep down underwater
where a living being such as myself
could never hope to survive.
And we have not survived.
You at least have not survived.
And the question remains:
am I somewhat to blame for your absence?
The least I might expect from you,
leaving all else aside,
is an answer to that one.
And I am still waiting.

If there is a knot –
and there surely must be –
it is impossible for me to untie it.
Take that for a given fact.
Do not blame me for what
you know I cannot do.
Sometimes I think to myself:
enough is enough.
There are clean lines to be attended to,
and a certain freshness in the wind.
I recognise this then to be my moment.
Jewels – of what preciousness? I wonder to myself –
hang pendent in the air. I stretch my mouth wide.
I howl with pleasure in front of the curtains, yanked open.
I watch the day drift easefully in front of me.
There is nothing I cannot seize.
I step back then, into the shadow
again, and wonder at my presumption.
I feel heavier on my legs.
My body slumps a little.
As if I were an antique column,

the cracks would be appearing.
Needless to say, you are there,
firm hand on my shoulder,
drawing me back to unease and sobriety.

At the cost of what pleasure?
How much can be measured
when so much is intangible?
And the situation only worsens,
the harder one looks into it.
And yet there is no alternative
unless the mind shuts down altogether.

Costs weigh upon me today,
how the mind lists and leans
in such unfavourable weather.
What is to be done about it all?
Nothing. This rent in the gauze
leads precisely to nowhere.
Nor would I have wanted it to happen,

not in such circumstances as these,
because the queues for the breakfast room
are intolerable again, and I find myself
hanging back, and dreaming
of looking out for you
because you are everywhere and nowhere
yet again and this is all a measure of human feeling,
though why I wish to bring this up
I have simply no idea because the bus stop
is just around the next corner, and I know that for a fact.
There is egg everywhere, on shirt and collar,
and I am frankly disgusted by my life.
I would suggest that you absent yourself
because I am no longer fit to be spoken to.
You already have, you explain to me,
with the utmost patience, and I stand in front of you then
without once looking up, though I do
recognise the shoes because I gave them to you
as a gift, one of so many, when we were
in our young prime, one September morning,
Lago di Maggiore,
the words do sound so wonderful,
as they always were, and must surely always be
as long as I remember it to have happened
to the two of us together, in that place
of such epiphanies. Do I now make myself
sound ridiculous? You always called me ridiculous,
and I have to admit you have a point.
My point though, is that we must not be too ready
to relinquish it all. All continues, does it not, to be set so fair
in memory and emotion. Something like that.
Could you put it better, were I to ask?
Would you be willing once again
to rise to our occasion, be that *declarative*
there is such a word in our rather pinched vocabulary?
Yes, I do still weep for you.
I cannot stop myself. You are my child, are you not?
You are perhaps what I never was, and never could have been.

The light came on just then, of its own accord.
I have no idea why things happen when they happen.
It is all a muddle and a mystification,
always has been, ever since that day
when my bicycle got stolen, and I stood there,
helpless, breasting the wind,
arms outstretched like a miniature scarecrow,
waiting for the birds to descend
and show some curiosity me-ward.
Needless to say, they were absent that day.
It all must begin again
after your jacket falls to the floor
with such apparent nonchalance.
Did you shrug it off by way of a warning?

Are there new tunes to be played on the organ?
Should we live out our lives all over again
as if scarcely anything had happened,
and we are raw innocents again,
burbling the usual nonsense,
smelling of toothpaste at mid-morning?
If this is what you want to ask me,
do go ahead. I have one foot in the car as usual,
impatient and eager to be gone,
but I can wait, I can withdraw it,
and even remove all the food from the boot
as if, all of a sudden, we have a change of plans,
and the entire cast of this burning day is different.
Can you see that too, now that I point it out to you?
Are you open to such a suggestion?
Or will you plead your usual somnolence
in the face of such challenges?
This is why you so unnerve and anger me,
so often. There is no keeping pace,
no hurry to be making the most or the best
of all that we are given.
And we have been given so much,
would you not have agreed,
had I ever had the courage to ask you?
So now, once again, it is I who am in the doldrums,
picking up dropped stitches
between hands which appear to wilt away
even as I stare down at them.
What has become of me?
What has become of the two of us?
Will no one say?
Has it always been too much to ask?

The new day begins with dropped pronouns in plenty.
There is a levelling hereabouts, a new sweeping away.
Consider how the street is whispering back at us.
All is at a slight angle to the true.
Where we you then when it all happened?

And where was I, more to the point,
so famous for the usual excuses?
I despair of you. I despair of things as they are.
It is all so common and lacklustre.
I for one would have preferred not to venture at all,
but such a choice was not mine to be made on that day,
and you, as usual, you wimp, were nowhere to be seen
when I posed the trickiest of questions.
Which was what exactly? I hear you asking.
And now your voice is echoing down the years,
your voice and mine together, we two dancing partners
who have never been so much alone as we are now.
I could take you back if you like,
lead you like a child, across water, light-stepping.
Could you manage that in your present condition?
Would I have the gall even to do it?
I have no idea why I am posing such questions.
It all feels so pitiful, and so unlikely
ever to be resolved, given the current state of things,
which are, in fact, not bad at all.
What miracle workers we are,
where all seemed so impossible,
and everything in contention.
I have sprung up again, it seems,
those new green shoots of spring
when everything seems to conspire together
to say yes and yes again, what a wonder,
my friend, that we were there at all,
and that I am here today,
listening so intently to all this eager talk?
How come, all at once, there can arrive
as if from nowhere this new Age of Promise?
Are the chords not gathered about us here
In the Piazza dei Promessi? Did you give
this place such a lovely name?
Did we make it all up between us?
Are we collaborating on our two brief lives
of make-believe as in the olden days?

I have no wish to take no for an answer.
You know how things are between us.
You are not into deep-rooted betrayal.
Your smile never allowed for it.
There was always, admit it, the cosy corner,
where old enmities fell away,
and those cruel accidents of the past
simply never happened.
I want you to believe all this,.
I want you to swear to it, solemnly,
with the two of us standing together,
shoulder to shoulder, in front of
the master of ceremonies
into whose gentle hands we have agreed
to commit ourselves here and hereafter.
Is that way too much to ask of you?
But did we not ask that already,
and then lose all the paperwork
when the ceiling came down?
Is that how you remember it?
And, if so, why must you always reduce everything
to ridicule in the end?
Is it that you were made that way,
and just cannot help yourself?
I'm sick of all this.
I'm tired of asking so many questions
when the answers are always so partial
and so comprehensively unsatisfactory.

Let's walk instead. The air smells good again.
The garden is proposing its usual favours.
The moment of questioning saunters by.
Didn't we make it this way, come on,
exactly as it is this morning?
Should we not call it a scene to die for?
You know me for what I am, which is why
you have just turned to look at me in the usual way,
with a measure of surprise,

as if I am something wholly new in your life,
and have said as much – blurted it out – with the usual bluntness.
(There's bacon grease to slip on, so watch your step.)
Except that I have not quite believed you.
It's nothing other than that familiar routine of yours.
I could have spotted it approaching from a mile away.
The words came out too pat,
as if there were no premeditation of any kind.
Am I accusing you of insincerity then?
Neither of had asked to live this long.
Neither of us had insisted upon
quite this level of commitment.
Which is why I am not insisting on it now.
Quite the opposite, in fact.
I am neither a fanatic nor a quitter.
Put one foot down here, and another there.
Look out for the worms!
Flower-pot banter is what you used to call it.
There was always a certain amount of exasperation,
as if we were both – both! – revving the engine
without actually going anywhere.
Witless behaviour – or not?
It all depends upon how fond you are of the very idea of us.
The jury's still out on that one.
So let's work on a settled routine for a change.
Let's, say, try and connive at our present and future happiness.
Isn't that as far as we need to go?
Couldn't that count as a worthy goal?
Did anyone ask for anything different?
Haven't we enough time to spare left between us?
Or are we both over-spent,
with our pockets helplessly turned inside out?
Perhaps I was a child before you were.

This is the side street I was counting on,
with the usual gang of listless strangers,
hopelessly perplexed, and on a hiding to nowhere.
Are we amongst them? Were we ever, once?

Do you recognise us there?
Have you preserved the picture in your head,
as if your mother had bequeathed you
that precious cameo at last, and you had collapsed at her feet,
weeping over her fidelity, at long last, you-ward?
I could have said as much of anyone
had I had the gumption,
which has been in such short supply.
It's a measure of our cruelty to each other,
this yearning to dig away, again and again,
at everything that was said to have happened,
this need for it all to be wrenched up to the light,
and then turned and turned about –
what a heartless endeavour!
Did we ever see each other for what we really were?
I never got the measure of all this craziness,
speaking for myself, of course – well, who else is there
when you come to tot up all the various columns?

And yet there is still some majesty hereabouts.
The air is so bright-shining once again, and especially so
when we walk up The Mall arm in arm,
leaning into each other,
incubating the brightest and the best of our lazy tunes,
savouring the last stench of the horses.
Was it all taken away all at once?
Did we, one winter morning, wake up with a start,
naked and mewling, fearing what the world
might do to us, if we did not run away to the mountains?
You always hated mountains, so that was never an option.
What was to be done then? You tell me.
I've practically run out of answers.
How do you turn a few random decisions
into a description of a life worthy to have been lived?
Was that the philosophical question
that pressed down upon us with such urgency,
just like being under the full weight
of a Sumo wrestler? Am I being disgusting now?
Or even racist?
I wish I still knew you as well as I know myself,.
which is perhaps scarcely at all.

And then there was that one, I mean.
And we patiently took it apart
as if it were an old-style watch,
waiting goodness how long
for any outcome that might please us.
What exactly did we expect that to be?
Did you get all those Anglo-Saxon riddles?
Did they make any sense to you?
Did they even please you as works of literary merit?
They passed me by – why pretend otherwise?
I was far too happy with a range of collar and ties
from the dark depths of the wardrobe
until I quickly grew up into something loucher and gutsier
altogether. But that was just me, wasn't it?
I'm not pretending to speak for anyone else,

and especially not these days
when there is such a range of options
available to be shuffled.
Does that make me a pack man then?
Why not? I have been called worse.
Once I was shredded so badly
that no amount of paper and glue
could re-assemble the bits of me.
It's not that they didn't try.
There was an entire team of experts
pinched together along the length of the sofa.
I was pacing back and forth in front of them
as if it was I who had been given the option
to choose for a change. Needless to say,
I sent them all away with a sandwich
and minimal expenses. Why not?
I got away with it – as with so much else.
This is what happens when you are awake
and forever open to new possibilities.
You don't have to nod to be alive.
That must be a lesson for us all,
and I am so glad to share it.
So few of us have such an acknowledged capacity for generosity.
Count me amongst the blessed then
f you have the abacus handy.
 know how old-fashioned you always tend to be
when matters of taste roar around the bend again.
'm happy to please you (but perhaps you know that already).
t makes for an easier life, wouldn't you agree?
This then is the life we have always lived.
 am happy to chronicle it, with due care,
so that there need be no misunderstanding between us.
 want all the measuring to be just so.
 want it all to come out clean and well calibrated –
 s do you, of course, I fondly surmise.
 e now, how I have upended the sack.
 here is nothing left to discover.
 e can both choose to relax again

because there are no secrets left between us.
Does all this sound like make-believe?
Well, that is exactly what poetry is,
a strange hazarding of words,
in which the familiar jostles so pleasingly
with the wholly unfamiliar, a kind of
guessing game driven by pure passion –
just like an old two-stroke engine at which we all
gape in wonderment, scarcely believing it
(and much else) to be alive in this world any more.
Come on now! Do something for a change.
I cannot be your beast of burden.
I wasn't built with such a capacity
for pride and wonderment.
You need to take life as it comes.
(After all, there are all the losses and gains to be balanced.)
Either that or the Beefcake Men
will haul you out of your seat in the gods
and fling you head first into the midden.
Imagine that for your most favoured option.

Do I really want life to be as it once was?
Is it history I so hanker after?
Are there books of truth-telling
to be gathered from the ditches
as I saunter along,
scrabbling through pockets of rubble,
so that I don't go astray again,
clutching the wrong hold-all
at the wrong bus station, and wailing meanwhile:
why am I back here anyway,
separated so cruelly
from my first pack of sandwiches?
This was never the answer.
It never qualified as either leave-taking
or home-coming. Tell me to my face.
In fact, I did not recognise its status.
I had my scowl set against it from the beginning,

ignorant and ever proud to be so.
Welcome to this world we have cobbled together!
And now, having just said all that,
you pop up like a circus routine
and tell me: relax, monster! You have gone too far!
Two old pennies only separate you from happiness.

Are you a joker, to laugh at me? Here's what happened.
I drew some lines in the dirt yesterday, at random,
measuring it all out, inch by inch,
trying to determine what would take me
from A to B and back again,
by the shortest possible route,
making Life seem – on the surface at least –
a little easier for myself.
And it worked, for as long as I drew
in the dirt with that stick I was holding.
It seemed to control me. It knew where it was going.
And I was happy to be drawn into a future
both determined and wholly unknown to me.
I was happy to recognise that there was
such pleasure to be gained
from all that seemingly random patterning.
I quickly bought into the narrative
that I might after all have been chosen –
by who though? Goodness only knows –
as a favoured child of destiny.

Twilight. It was then, as light fell, that I opened
the box and breathed into it
words of promise and concern
before quickly sealing it again with duct tape.
Had I a plan in mind?
I was open to any and every possibility again.
When a letter arrives, seemingly in order to rule things out,
you rise up like a conqueror to reclaim the ground.
That was my attitude, as it had always been.
I stepped into the box in order to reclaim my own life.

There were qualifications, as in the case of any life,
matters to be ruled on, reasons for not walking
in the same direction as the next man.
All came together at once until we shuffled, piecemeal, away,
and began conversations in tongues hitherto unknown
to all of us barring one or two. It is, in short,

the well-spring that matters most of all.
But were we all ready at the source,
equal to that day's venture? I asked him that again,
and he chose not to answer, being sneery.
Is this the first? he asked, as if we were posing once again
as strangers to each other, which was, of course, an absurdity.
The roads seemed solid enough to the touch of the foot,
but who knows what might eventuate when
two come together as one? What sealant known to man
can lend its strength to such a relationship as ours?

There were some days – haphazard if you like –
when they all came along, and in such good order too,
patient as lambs, and so ready, when speedily invited,
to step onto the jetty, and stride on ahead
with such a boldness of tread,
to test the waves and how they looked,
their violent oncoming
on any fresh September morning such as that one.
How we lived our lives to the full in those days!
It seems scarcely credible now
when the wind has buffeted us
in so many different directions at once,
enough and more to make us all dizzy
until the end of time and beyond,
did you not say to me, quite casually,
  seem to recall, only yesterday…
in fact, was not that the chorus line –
until the end of time and beyond –
so readily shared amongst us?
Needless to say, it was at such times
that we two hung back, in the grip of self-doubt.
wanted it to be like that. It felt right, if not consolatory.
We were a heap of crushed egg shells,
and it was of such that our tender love then consisted
  I am not rudely mistaken.
Which I am, you now say,
nudging me from behind

and shouting at me to wake up
from the usual catalogue of follies.
My friend, go to it then. You have the pills
at your full disposal, the plumb line, and the thread.
That is as much as you will ever need and,
though you do recognise it now,
it is all that I have already given you,
my gift to you, in your hour of need.

You see, I have been helpless for so long,
not knowing in which direction to turn
to find you again, all the time recognising full well
that you were not to be found at all
because I had already sifted the fineness
of all that there remained of you
through the spaces between my fingers,
and I still remember so well
that you amounted to so little that morning,
and that the entire world agreed with me,
all those who walked by without even
knowing or noticing what was happening.
Do not blame them for their indifference.
Who knows what glue binds one to another?
Who has ever taken its tacky measure between thumb and finger?
I for one have lived my life in perfect contentment
because I have reduced the whole rackety fandango
to such a tight and meagre outcome.
That is the best way to avoid disappointment.
These houses understand it – see the way
they seem to lean into each other,
as if proffering friendship. Or protection.

They need such protection because bricks, mortar,
in fact, all that we make of this world as it is,
breathes and lives just as we do.
I have learnt much from houses.
They have had much to teach me.
I have, for example, become anchoritic

by nature these several gone days,
a brick for my pillow, and mortar for my daily portion,
waking to face the desert, calling out with
such long and plaintive cries of desolation
towards the empty, thirsting spaces,
boundless within myself in the way that
these spaces beyond this fragile body of mine
are boundless in their turn…
Motionless, I move beyond myself –
It is a miracle that I am describing.
I do believe in miracles in so far as they apply to myself.
I am a paradigm of the uttermost foolishness.

It is so easy to be known, that's what I tell myself.
Put yourself out there, with a slow turn of the leg,
and see who watches. The stones watch.
They listen to your breathing.
Were you two miles from nowhere
when it happened, that she spoke to you again?
The glass, did it shatter? And then you both looked up,
as if it were a matter of some consequence?
All these recollections are a losing game,
a catch-as-catch-can, a makeshift business.
As is climbing out of bed when the sun rises.
I asked you once about everything that is,
being of a philosophical bent that morning.
You merely shrugged it off, of course.
How better to deal with me?
And then we returned to speaking of
the movement, the sheer, headlong unpredictability
of swallows, and of how they consumed us
beside the lake that evening. Yes, what an
evening that had been! Their nest
seemed to hang in the eaves, tucked away,
es, just beyond reach of our seeing.
they would swoop across and then back,
 if life itself depended upon it.
Meanwhile the ducks were asleep

on the wooden pontoon beneath
that wearily bucked and heaved in the water.
It was a regular, lulling motion
that seemed to synchronise so well with the evening light,
the way it fell, and the way we would raise our glasses
to each other from time to time, as if in
pleased acknowledgement of our presences there.

I was never there, you know.
I am imagining this life for myself,
a more vivid and engaging version
of all that I have been, to myself and to you.
It consoles me, you see,
it consoles me for your absence.
Your very stillness makes it possible
for me to speak so slowly to you
because you will no longer find my hesitations
wearisome, as you always used to do.
You will never try to leave,
wrenching yourself up out of your seat,
in pursuit of a more positive outcome.

I wanted you to leave, you know,
although I never told you so
because I wanted my life to be
a prolonged exercise in brave self-sufficiency,
as my father's had once been,
God bless all those who knew him.
I never did. He passed me by on the other side.
He had been a model of a man
to all intents and purposes.
I am of a warrior caste after all then.
Let us nail that down
so that no one can deny the truth of it.

Such absurdities. I can scarcely believe
that I am using such words.
You would be within your rights to laugh at them.

In the beginning, there was so much laughter between us.
You stood, that first time, as if posing for a photograph
that would never be taken. Who is to blame for that?
Is not each and every one of us responsible
for the eking out of his own vanities?
Was I worse? Did I even try to make a comely shape?
And what age were we anyway?
Such a deal of imponderables
that I have been telling myself
as I stand out here on the step this morning,
and conjure that lane down which we used to walk,
often stumbling, because it was so steep and so twisty.
Sometimes you took my hand, because even then,
even when very young, I was not so steady.
Did you believe in me? By which I probably mean:
believe that I existed? To the extent that
I believed in you – if, that is, I did?
Is that also open to question?
Is not the entire world so open-ended
that this conversation must surely go nowhere
in the end, whenever the end, forever so elusive,
may chance upon us? You tell *me* for a change.
I have had enough. I want to quieten things down
at least for a day or two, old friend, if that's how
I can conceive of you. It is all too much to bear,
one day heaped upon another
like so much baggage tossed into a hole,
and then never retrieved by its owner.
There is so little kindness in these parts,
so little to soothe us, so little to take away
the pain of it all.

When the cards were dealt out that morning,
we sat opposite each other, cross-legged,
knees almost touching. You had bruisings
you would never explain, that I have never forgotten.
I had a way of dealing the pack that so impressed you.
I always wanted to impress you. Did I ever tell you that?

We played for the hell of it, hours at a time,
saying almost nothing, looking down.
Your hair was a sandy brown, as if dusted.
I wanted to blow that dust away,
but I never had the courage.
I seldom possessed the courage
to seize hold of the moment.
It was always as if I was being lifted,
quite gently for the most part,
and carried along to the next occasion,
where I would open my eyes
to find myself there, and respond, as seemed fit,
with the usual shyness.
I was never in command of my life.
It always proved to be a fearful venture,
hazardings in plenty,
and a catalogue of disappointments.
I might say that I never wanted you
to be the ultimate disappointment
because, were that to happen,
I would surely have been the cause of it.
Why would I contemplate such a thing
when your smile seemed to hold such promise?
That is as much as there is then.
There are footprints still to be considered,
notes to be read that may not even be found
within the time available to me.
I am looking. I am always looking.
I tell myself that I have travelled far
in pursuit of what happened.
There are various prolonged conversations
with sympathetic participants to be added to the mix.
It is still so much a tangle, which amounts to
a provocation, of course.

Whose truth do you opt for?
The cat left the house again today,
our natural wanderer.

No, it would not be right to say
as much as needs to be said
because you would not tolerate
all that dinning in the ear.
Say it out loud then.
Throw off the last disguise,
the thrift-shop wig of unruly hair.
I am not Rimbaud, you once said.
My world is unnatural to me.
We have that in common then.
It makes no sense any more,
even to lift up this spoon and talk to you again.
The table is bare. The shops are all closed
against me. The man is waiting at the door
to check my credentials.
I could give him my voice
as a gesture of amity,
and see how he fared
in the future, his future, ours.
If I recognised his face,
matters might be a little easier.
There are of course all these books
as consolation prizes.
I am handing them out now, to all and sundry.
Join the patient ones in the queue.
One day you became my best of enemies,
and that fear of you has kept me going,
that you would catch me out,
turn me into someone I did not even recognise.
Perhaps I do need mother at the bedside this morning,
tea cup astir, rattling in its saucer.
I walked away from there too,
just as quickly as I was able.
It was such a refreshment,
to be rid of all that I had been.
And then came entire worlds of conjuring,
night after night on that stage
alongside all those other *voyous*,

57

with so little other than this agony
of enforced improvisation
by way of consolation.
You recognise this kind of thing, of course.
It is your old, familiar patch all over again.
Nothing comes as a surprise to you.
Kick out a leg. Make it all brazen,
as I have tended to do, wouldn't you agree?

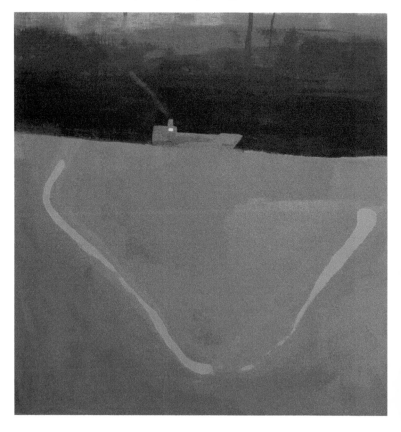

What would you ask of me?
What would you like me to do for you,
given these particular circumstances?
I am as clean as all my clothes.
In the aftermath of the current venture,
I may take a stroll as far as the corner,
merely to look at the world.

Two or three may still know me.
Who said I do not live in hope?
The basket is, as usual, half empty.
Asking could be an answer,
entirely random I mean,
questions plucked out of the hat,
tiny, crumpled balls of wrapping paper
containing the darkest truths
ever to be fathomed by man,
that debased and helpless creature…

Join me now for the conversation.
There are chairs still to be added.
This pool hall is infinitely expandable,
and others are waiting in the wings.
Other halls, that is. I would not accept
that there could be more of us.
You have not yet asked me for a light
this morning. Is that because you have
kicked the habit at last?
Were you left with multiple bruisings?
Are you on a health drive today?
I would describe the weather,
were you to ask, as medium mild,
with the promise of balmy breezes
for the more poetical occasions.
For which, of course, I shall be preparing myself.
You do want me to be like this, don't you?
You want me to inhabit the Writing Life,
not least because the very idea is such as joke?
Frankly, nothing ever happens.
Who has ever complained
about the racket made by the movement
of this innocent pen of mine,
a pen so full of wiles
that no one could possibly understand
what creature pushed it so gaily along?
Is this a game of insouciance then?

Call it what you like as long as you have breath.
You will have my full support.
I have nothing left to lose
now that they have ripped up
the last length of branch line
that once served this stretch of the coast.
We are so isolated out here,
between the railway track and the wetlands,
with only a fleeting songbird for company.
Would you like me to introduce you to my habitat?
It may come to seem familiar to you by and by.
More remarkable things have happened.
There are leaps of faith to be made.
It is not all severe black charcoal lines,
crude divisions of a single sheet of paper.
I was never happy to enjoy things by halves.
Your prognostications, pompous or not,
need not be so unwelcome.
Will that make for a beginning of sorts?
Would you be prepared to countenance such a proposal?
Well then. Speak up for a change.
Don't bang on about the last gasp known to man.
I for one have never believed
that there would not be an outcome
favourable somehow or other
to both of us or neither.
You only need to say. So say it. Don't hold back.
You only need to venture a word – or a foot,
out of doors, just over the threshold
of, aah, untold possibilities…
And then on, at least as far as hell's mouth.
Or beyond, if you would prefer that.
I'll make space for your venturesomeness.
Why not? Who else have I to lose?
And so I say it again: a single footfall will do.
And then, after that, your old-time, favourite knock,
hammer-heavy as ever,
so keen to interrupt my favourite thoughts,

and then the usual blah,
just as if we were in mid-conversation,
before the weather got bad again,
and we both agreed to fall silent.